STEM STORIES

Space Exploration

FROM GALILEO GALILEI TO NEIL DEGRASSE TYSON

Jenny Mason

Checkerboard
Library

An Imprint of Abdo Publishing
abdopublishing.com

ABDOPUBLISHING.COM

Printed in the United States of America, North Mankato, Minnesota
052018
092018

 THIS BOOK CONTAINS RECYCLED MATERIALS

Design and production: Mighty Media, Inc.
Editor: Rebecca Felix
Cover Photographs: AP Images (right), Shutterstock (center, left)
Interior Photographs: Internet Archive Book Images/Flickr, p. 22; ITU Pictures/NASA/Flickr, p. 15; NASA, pp. 17, 29 (top); NASA Hubble Space Telescope/Flickr, p. 23; NASA/JPL-Caltech/MSSS, p. 27; NASA/Wikimedia Commons, p. 13; Shutterstock, pp. 4-5, 11, 25, 28 (bottom), 29 (bottom); Wikimedia Commons, pp. 7, 9, 19, 21, 28 (top)

Library of Congress Control Number: 2017961648

Publisher's Cataloging-in-Publication Data
Name: Mason, Jenny, author.
Title: Space Exploration: From Galileo Galilei to Neil deGrasse Tyson / by Jenny Mason.
Other titles: From Galileo Galilei to Neil deGrasse Tyson
Description: Minneapolis, Minnesota : Abdo Publishing, 2019. | Series: STEM stories |
     Includes online resources and index.
Identifiers: ISBN 9781532115493 (lib.bdg.) | ISBN 9781532156212 (ebook)
Subjects: LCSH: Space sciences--Juvenile literature. | Space exploration (Astronautics)--
     Juvenile literature. | Astronomy--History--Juvenile literature. | Inventors--
     Biography--Juvenile literature.
Classification: DDC 520.92--dc23

Contents

Exploring the Skies

Do you ever pretend your bike is a rocket booster as you ride it up a ramp and fly through the air? Have you ever floated in a pool, imagining what it's like for astronauts in zero gravity? You're not alone! People have dreamed of space exploration since ancient times.

Prehistoric **cultures** carved the sky's patterns onto bones and stones. Many ancient cultures used religion to explain the wonders in the sky. This included ancient Greeks, Egyptians, Mayans, and Chinese.

In the 1700s and 1800s, scientific tools helped people learn more about space. In the 1900s,

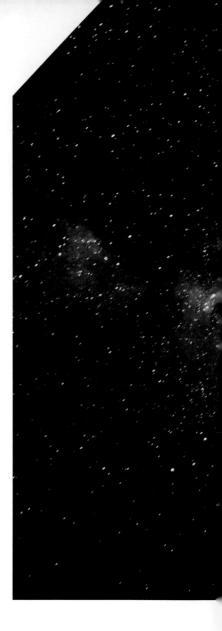

scientists built spacecraft bound for actual space travel. Later that century, the first humans traveled into space!

From the earliest space researchers to today's daring explorers, humankind has learned a lot about our **galaxy** and beyond. And today's **technology** is allowing us to gain new information faster than ever. The story of space exploration begins and continues with the people who study, investigate, and experience it!

The Milky Way is the galaxy that holds our solar system.

CHAPTER 1

Star Gazing

Astronomy in some form dates back to the beginning of human history. Early evidence of this includes bones carved with the moon phases. These bones are thought to be from 30,000 BCE. Many ancient **cultures** also tracked the cycles of the moon and other celestial objects. Some cultures converted these cycles into calendars tracking the passage of time.

Historians believe the Mesopotamians began using a lunar calendar sometime between 3000 and 2000 BCE. Ancient Mayans, who lived between 1800 BCE and 250 CE, also used astronomy to create calendars.

By 550 BCE, ancient Greeks created drawings and models of how they thought the universe looked. In these artworks, the sun and a thin rim of stars spun around Earth. The universe was unchanging, meaning no new celestial bodies ever formed. Religion influenced this idea. The Greeks believed the god or gods who made the universe would not make anything imperfect. Greek models of the universe became the standard for many centuries.

In 1543 CE, Nicolaus Copernicus challenged common beliefs about space. Copernicus was a Polish astronomer. He studied the work of astronomers who came before him. From these studies, Copernicus determined that Earth and the other planets moved around the sun. People rejected this idea and **ridiculed** Copernicus. It was not until several **decades** later that another astronomer made discoveries to help support Copernicus's idea.

Copernicus believed a planet's distance from the sun affected the size of its orbit around the sun.

CHAPTER 2

Seeing Is Believing

In 1608, a German glasses maker patented the telescope. The device was made to see across long stretches of land or sea. In 1609, Galileo Galilei pointed a telescope at the night sky. Galileo was one of history's most important astronomers.

Galileo improved the telescope's design to see deeper into space. In doing so, he saw Jupiter had its own moons orbiting around it. This proved not all celestial bodies orbited Earth. Galileo also saw Venus was in shadow at different times, depending on where it was in relation to the sun. He realized this meant Venus orbited the sun, not Earth. This supported Copernicus's theory!

The Catholic Church condemned Galileo for his findings, which **contradicted** its beliefs about God and the universe. But not everyone criticized Galileo. Galileo invited others to use his telescope and see what he described. And, those who could afford the expensive device bought a telescope and saw for themselves. As a result, more people began to believe Galileo and change their ideas about space. This encouraged others to continue exploring.

Galileo Galilei

BORN: 1564, Pisa, Italy

DIED: 1642, Tuscany, Italy

FACT: Galileo was the oldest of six siblings. His father was a famous musician.

FACT: Galileo was an astronomer, engineer, mathematician, physicist, and philosopher.

FACT: Galileo discovered that the Milky Way **galaxy** was not a cloud, but a sea of stars.

ACHIEVEMENTS

▶ Galileo believed theories needed lots of testing through controlled experiments. His habit became the standard common scientific practice. But it was unusual at the time. Because of this, Galileo is often considered the father of modern science.

▶ Galileo used math to **predict** exactly how long a **pendulum** might swing. This paved the way for making **accurate** clocks.

▶ Galileo's findings helped support Copernicus's theory that Earth moved around the sun.

▶ Some of Galileo's experiments later helped British scientist Sir Isaac Newton explain gravity.

STEM Star

CHAPTER 3

Expanding Understanding

Galileo also performed experiments that influenced space exploration. One was dropping items from great heights to learn about their behavior as they fell. Galileo discovered that a dropped item's **acceleration** was constant, measurable, and **predictable**. This helped British scientist Sir Isaac Newton study motion in the 1660s.

Newton saw an apple fall from a tree. He wondered why it fell down and not up or to the side. Newton used this question to study gravity. Gravity is a pulling force in all objects. The Earth pulls on apples, and the apples pull on Earth. But the bigger an object, the harder it pulls. Therefore, Earth pulls harder on a falling apple, bringing it to the ground.

Newton came up with three laws of motion for all objects in the universe. First, an object not in motion will remain still until another force acts upon it. An object in motion will continue moving until another force slows it down or speeds it up. Second, if the same force is applied to two objects of different masses, the

Newton was best known for his laws of motion and work on gravity. But he studied many other topics as well, such as light, mathematics, and religion.

one with more mass will move more slowly. More mass equals less speed. Third, for every action, there is an equal but opposite reaction.

This information affected the way people studied space in coming centuries. In the 1900s, people began thinking of traveling into space. Newton's laws influenced how they would get there.

CHAPTER 4

Problem-Solving Space Travel

As scientific study of space grew more advanced, so did people's imaginations. By the 1930s, many writers had dreamed up tales of space travel. That same **decade**, the Soviet Union began a space program with the goal of traveling into space. The United States began its own space program, the National Aeronautics and Space Administration (NASA), in the 1950s.

Later that decade, a rocket scientist from each organization had similar ideas to make spacecraft like those in fiction. These men were Wernher von Braun and Sergei Pavlovich Korolev. Von Braun worked for NASA and Korolev for the Soviet Union space program. Both men raced to be first to launch a spacecraft.

Von Braun and Korolev were both familiar with Newton's theories of gravity. They knew a spacecraft would need to escape Earth's orbit in order to enter space. Scientists had determined an object must travel

FUN FACT

Modern space shuttles carry about 4 million pounds (1.8 million kg) of fuel!

25,000 miles per hour (40,200 kmh) to do this. Fuel would set the spacecraft in motion. But getting enough power to reach high speeds meant using a lot of fuel. More fuel equaled more mass. And more mass equals less speed. Scientists needed to solve this problem if space travel was ever going to leave the ground.

Wernher von Braun later became director of NASA's Marshall Space Flight Center. He developed several spacecraft during his career.

CHAPTER 5

To Infinity and Beyond

The Soviet space program experienced years of tests and failures. Despite these challenges, on October 4, 1957, it successfully launched the first space **probe**, Sputnik. This was history's first human-made object in space. On April 12, 1961, the program also sent the first human into space! Yuri Gagarin traveled on a rocket into space and orbited Earth for 108 minutes.

The Soviets' success spurred the United States to increase its space travel efforts. The two nations had been **allies** during **World War II**. But when the war ended, they experienced tension that lasted more than 40 years. This period was called the Cold War. Both countries competed to have the best **technology** during this time. Their space programs were a major part of this competition.

NASA hurried to send an American into space. Just 23 days after Gagarin's trip, NASA succeeded. On May 5, 1961, it sent US astronaut Alan B. Shepard into the sky on a spacecraft. Shepard soared over Earth and returned in 15 minutes.

Yuri Gagarin entered space on the *Vostok 1*. Upon return, the spacecraft ejected him so he could land by parachute.

NASA used computers to accomplish this flight. But these computers were not machines. They were African-American women with incredible math skills! In the 1960s, these women computed the equations to help launch, navigate, and land US spacecraft.

CHAPTER 6

Moon Mission

In July 1969, NASA sent the first humans to the moon. They were astronauts Edwin "Buzz" Aldrin, Michael Collins, and Neil Armstrong. NASA completed several more moon missions in the 1970s. It also explored other celestial locations. Instead of humans, robots made these trips. These machines are safer to launch, because no lives are lost if they crash in space.

Searching for signs of **extraterrestrial** life became a major goal for robots in space. In 1977, NASA sent *Voyager 1* and *Voyager 2* to study the outer solar system. These **probes** had cameras, sound recorders, and other instruments to gather data.

Each probe also carried a gold plate. US astronomer Carl Sagan led a team of scientists in designing these plates. One side of each had symbols revealing Earth's **cosmic** address. The other sides held images and sound recordings such as music and animal noises. Scientists hoped that if extraterrestrials existed and found one of these plates, it would communicate to them information about Earth. The probes are still traveling through space today.

Aldrin walks on the surface of the moon on July 20, 1969.

CHAPTER 7

NASA Space Shuttles

By the 1980s, launching robotic spacecraft was a regular practice for NASA. But NASA still sent people into space as well. On April 12, 1981, NASA launched a space shuttle program. The program's mission was to send spacecraft to and from space with less waste. Previous spacecraft were usually so damaged from travel that they were trashed upon return. The shuttles would also launch **satellites** and act as space laboratories.

NASA constructed a reusable shuttle fleet. Each shuttle was attached to a large rocket. A shuttle launched on a rocket and landed on a runway upon return. Then, the shuttle could be strapped to a new rocket and re-launched. Each shuttle could also hold 11 astronauts, where previous NASA spacecraft only held 3.

The *Columbia* was the first shuttle flown. It completed seven successful shuttle missions over the next five years. Then, on January 6, 1986, another shuttle, called *Challenger*, took off for a mission. Seventy-three seconds later, the spacecraft exploded. Everyone onboard died.

After the *Challenger* incident, the space shuttle program was grounded for three years. During this time, NASA engineers worked to improve shuttle safety measures. The space shuttle program ran for 30 years. In this time, it completed 135 missions.

An investigation was done to figure out why *Challenger* exploded. Researchers learned two rings used to separate sections of the rocket booster malfunctioned due to cold air temperatures.

CHAPTER 8

Amazing Spacecraft

NASA's space shuttle program enabled many astronauts to explore space. In 1990, it also carried the most powerful telescope ever developed into orbit. The space shuttle *Discovery* carried the Hubble Space Telescope into Earth's orbit. This brought the device beyond the haze of the planet's atmosphere. Because of this, the telescope could see much farther and take clearer pictures of deep space than all other earthbound telescopes.

The Hubble discovered 1,500 new **galaxies**. It took photos of stars and nebulas, which are dust clouds where stars form. The Hubble also captured images of **supernovas**. This was the first time many of these space **phenomena** were seen by humans. The Hubble still orbits Earth today.

In 1998, the International Space Station (ISS) was launched into orbit. Several European countries, Japan, Canada, Russia, and the United States joined together to build this huge spacecraft. Larger than a football field, the station had to be carried in pieces and assembled in space!

The International Space Station orbits about 248 miles (399 km) above Earth.

Once the ISS was completed, scientists from around the world traveled to it for research missions. The scientists lived onboard, studying space and zero gravity. Scientists continue to travel to and stay onboard the orbiting ISS today.

Telescopes:
PAST AND PRESENT

Early telescopes were tubes with two lenses. The ocular lens was in the eyepiece. The objective lens was nearest the object being viewed. The modern Hubble Space Telescope has a similar design. But the Hubble uses mirrors instead of lenses, has advanced parts, and is very powerful.

GALILEO'S TELESCOPES

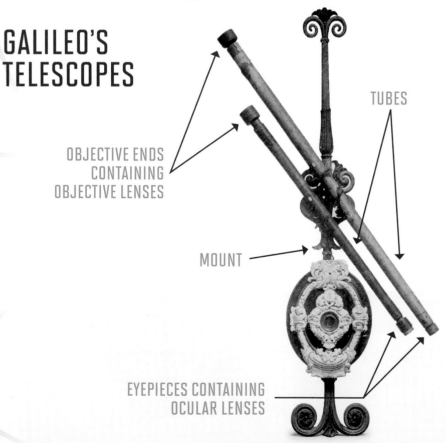

TUBES

OBJECTIVE ENDS
CONTAINING
OBJECTIVE LENSES

MOUNT

EYEPIECES CONTAINING
OCULAR LENSES

HUBBLE SPACE TELESCOPE

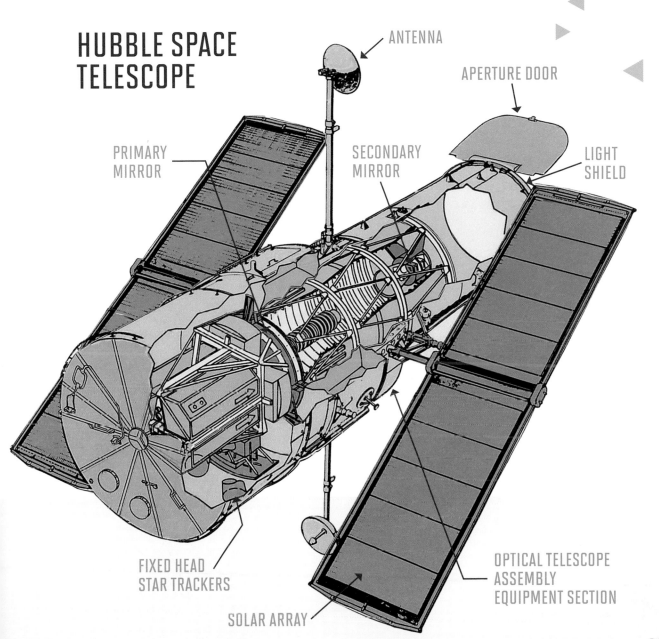

ANTENNA

APERTURE DOOR

PRIMARY MIRROR

SECONDARY MIRROR

LIGHT SHIELD

FIXED HEAD STAR TRACKERS

OPTICAL TELESCOPE ASSEMBLY EQUIPMENT SECTION

SOLAR ARRAY

CHAPTER 9

Examining Planets

As scientists explored the sky from the ISS, others made space discoveries on Earth. One discovery concerned Pluto. Some scientists decided it was not large enough to be a true planet. They said Pluto was a dwarf planet. Scientists disagreed about this for years. In 2000, **astrophysicist** Neil deGrasse Tyson brought this disagreement into the global spotlight.

Tyson is the director of New York City's Hayden Planetarium. He labeled Pluto as a dwarf planet in a new display there. This sparked global **controversy**. At first, scientists argued against Tyson. But many later agreed with him. In 2006, the International Astronomical Union voted that Pluto was no longer a planet.

Tyson became known as a space expert. Many people think he explains space topics in a way that is easy to understand, inspiring people's interest in space. This interest includes reading about space, viewing photos of space, and more. Today, even people who are not astronauts hope to one day visit another planet!

Neil deGrasse Tyson

BORN: October 5, 1958, New York City, New York

FACT: Tyson visited Hayden Planetarium at age nine. He became fascinated by space and made studying it his life's work.

FACT: Tyson has many jobs. He is an **astrophysicist**, author, and TV show and **podcast** host.

FACT: Tyson has published 13 books about space.

ACHIEVEMENTS

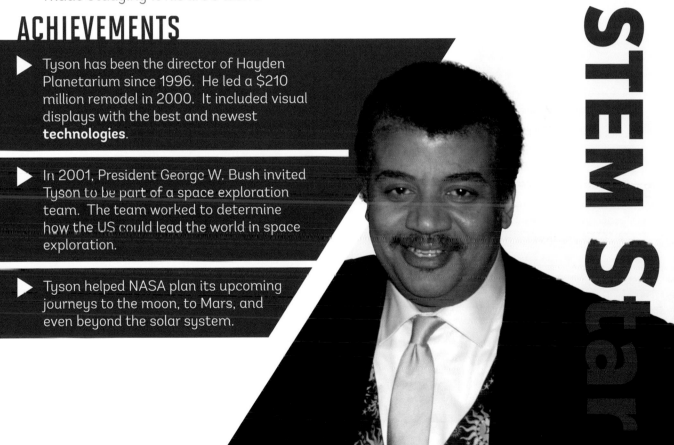

▶ Tyson has been the director of Hayden Planetarium since 1996. He led a $210 million remodel in 2000. It included visual displays with the best and newest **technologies**.

▶ In 2001, President George W. Bush invited Tyson to be part of a space exploration team. The team worked to determine how the US could lead the world in space exploration.

▶ Tyson helped NASA plan its upcoming journeys to the moon, to Mars, and even beyond the solar system.

STEM Star

CHAPTER 10

There's No Space Like Home

Throughout history, most space travelers have been professional astronauts. In 2004, a pilot entered space on *SpaceShipOne*, a spacecraft launched by US company Scaled Composites. The pilot flew this spacecraft into space and back in less than 30 minutes. Tickets for *SpaceShipTwo*, made to carry tourists, are on sale for $250,000 each. But space flights with tourists have yet to occur.

In recent years, building human communities on Mars has become a popular idea. This is because Mars is the most **habitable** planet after Earth. However, there is less gravity on Mars than on Earth. Research has shown living in low gravity can damage the human body. Over time, it can weaken bones and flatten eyeballs.

Also, space has high levels of **radiation** that can increase humans' risk of developing certain fatal illnesses. Scientists are working to make space travel safer. In 2017, Israeli scientists created AstroRad, a vest to protect space travelers' organs from radiation. US scientist Rainer Meinke is working on magnetic

NASA's *Curiosity* rover arrived on Mars in 2012 to study the planet. Since then, the rover has taken more than 400,000 photos. Most of these images are of the planet. But some are rover selfies!

fabric to wrap around a spaceship. This fabric would protect passengers from space **radiation** the same way Earth's magnetic field protects living things here.

The mysteries of space continue to fascinate people. Researchers, scientists, and space explorers face and solve new challenges every day. With these great minds at work, space may one day be our playground, or even our home!

Timeline

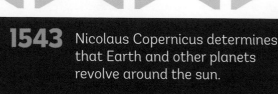

1543 Nicolaus Copernicus determines that Earth and other planets revolve around the sun.

1609 Galileo Galilei uses a telescope to study space. His observations support Copernicus's theory.

1660s Sir Isaac Newton works out three laws of motion for all objects in the universe.

1957 The Soviet Union launches Sputnik into orbit around Earth. The probe is the first human-made object in space.

1961 On April 12, Yuri Gagarin becomes the first human in space.

1969 In July, three US astronauts become the first humans on the moon.

1977 NASA launches *Voyager 1* and *Voyager 2* to explore the outer solar system.

1981 NASA launches its space shuttle program.

2006 The International Astronomical Union agrees with Neil deGrasse Tyson that Pluto is not a true planet.

2017 Scientists create AstroRad, a special vest space travelers can wear to protect themselves from radiation.

Glossary

acceleration—the act of moving faster or gaining speed.

accurate—free from error.

ally—a person, group, or nation united for some special purpose.

astrophysicist—a person who studies the behavior and measurements of objects outside Earth's atmosphere.

contradict—to say the opposite of a statement.

controversy—a discussion marked by strongly different views.

cosmic—of or relating to the universe in contrast to Earth alone.

culture—the customs, arts, and tools of a nation or a people at a certain time.

decade—a period of ten years.

extraterrestrial—coming from beyond Earth.

galaxy—a huge group of stars, planets, and other space objects.

habitable—safe and good enough for people to live in.

pendulum—a body suspended from a fixed point so as to swing freely under gravity.

phenomena—facts or events that are rare or extraordinary.

podcast—a program that is like a radio or television show but that is downloaded over the internet.

predict—to guess about something in advance using observation, experience, or reasoning. Something that can be guessed about this way is predictable.

probe—a device used to explore and send back information.

radiation—the act or process of giving out light, heat, electricity, or other radiant energy.

ridicule—to laugh at or make fun of someone in an unkind way.

satellite—a manufactured object that orbits Earth. It relays scientific information back to Earth.

supernova—a star that suddenly becomes very bright because it explodes.

technology (tehk-NAH-luh-jee)—machinery and equipment developed for practical purposes using scientific principles and engineering.

World War II—from 1939 to 1945, fought in Europe, Asia, and Africa. Great Britain, France, the United States, the Soviet Union, and their allies were on one side. Germany, Italy, Japan, and their allies were on the other side.

Online Resources

Booklinks
NONFICTION NETWORK
FREE! ONLINE NONFICTION RESOURCES

To learn more about space exploration, visit **abdobooklinks.com**. These links are routinely monitored and updated to provide the most current information available.

Index